MacAulay, Kelley.
What are flowers? /
2013.

bk   08/05/14

What are flowers?

by Kelley MacAulay

🌱 Crabtree Publishing Company
www.crabtreebooks.com

Author
Kelley MacAulay

Publishing plan research and development
Reagan Miller, Crabtree Publishing Company

Editorial director
Kathy Middleton

Editors
Reagan Miller, Crystal Sikkens

Proofreader
Kelly McNiven

Notes to adults
Reagan Miller

Photo research
Crystal Sikkens

Design
Ken Wright

**Production coordinator
and prepress technician**
Ken Wright

Print coordinator
Margaret Amy Salter

Photographs
Thinkstock: pages 13, 19, 24 (nectar)
Wikimedia Commons: ForestWander: page 17
Other images by Shutterstock

Library and Archives Canada Cataloguing in Publication

MacAulay, Kelley, author
    What are flowers? / Kelley MacAulay.

(Plants close-up)
Includes index.
Issued in print and electronic formats.
ISBN 978-0-7787-1286-2 (bound).--ISBN 978-0-7787-0016-6 (pbk.).--
ISBN 978-1-4271-9372-8 (pdf).--ISBN 978-1-4271-9368-1 (html)

    1. Angiosperms--Juvenile literature. 2. Flowers--Juvenile
literature. I. Title. II. Series: Plants close-up

QK653.M23 2013   j582.13   C2013-904033-1
                                             C2013-904034-X

Library of Congress Cataloging-in-Publication Data

MacAulay, Kelley.
    What are flowers? / Kelley MacAulay.
       p. cm. -- (Plants close-up)
    Includes index.
    ISBN 978-0-7787-1286-2 (reinforced library binding) -- ISBN 978-0-7787-0016-6
(pbk.) -- ISBN 978-1-4271-9372-8 (electronic pdf) -- ISBN 978-1-4271-9368-1
(electronic html)
    1. Flowers--Juvenile literature. I. Title. II. Series: Plants close-up.

QK49.M175 2013
580--dc23
                                             2013023435

Crabtree Publishing Company

www.crabtreebooks.com   1-800-387-7650

Printed in Hong Kong/092013/BK20130703

Copyright © **2014 CRABTREE PUBLISHING COMPANY.** All rights reserved. No part of this publication may be reproduced, stored in a retrieval system or be transmitted in any form or by any means, electronic, mechanical, photocopying, recording, or otherwise, without the prior written permission of Crabtree Publishing Company. In Canada: We acknowledge the financial support of the Government of Canada through the Canada Book Fund for our publishing activities.

Published in Canada
Crabtree Publishing
616 Welland Ave.
St. Catharines, Ontario
L2M 5V6

Published in the United States
Crabtree Publishing
PMB 59051
350 Fifth Avenue, 59th Floor
New York, New York 10118

Published in the United Kingdom
Crabtree Publishing
Maritime House
Basin Road North, Hove
BN41 1WR

Published in Australia
Crabtree Publishing
3 Charles Street
Coburg North
VIC 3058

Contents

Plant parts

Plants have different parts. Roots, stems, leaves, and flowers are all parts of plants. Each part has a job to do to help the plant stay alive and grow.

flowers

stem

leaves

roots

seeds

A flower's job is to make **seeds**.

Seeds grow into new plants.

Looking at flowers

Most plants have flowers. Some flowers are tiny. Other flowers are large. Flowers can grow in both hot and cold places. Crocuses grow in cold places.

Some plants grow only one flower. Other plants grow many flowers. Bluebells grow many flowers.

Tiny buds

Flowers grow inside **buds**. Buds grow at the tops of stems. A bud has tough, green leaves that form a closed ball to protect the flower. These leaves are called **sepals**.

buds

stem

sepals

As a flower grows, the sepals start to move apart and open up.

Parts called petals

The flower inside a bud has leaves called **petals**. Petals protect the inside parts of the flower. Petals are often bright colors.

petal

Some flowers have petals that are one color.

Others have petals that are many colors.

These orchids have yellow and pink petals.

Sweet nectar

Many flowers smell sweet. Bright petals and sweet smells attract birds and insects to flowers. **Nectar** is a sweet liquid found inside flowers. Bees collect nectar to make honey.

Birds and other insects drink nectar.
Hummingbirds have long beaks. Their
beaks reach nectar deep inside flowers.

Pollen

Pollen is also found inside flowers. Pollen is often yellow. It looks like yellow dust. Pollen can make some people sneeze.

A flower needs pollen from another flower of the same kind to make seeds. Plants cannot move from place to place. They depend on insects, birds, and other animals to bring them the pollen they need to make new seeds.

pollen

Moving pollen

Birds and insects can move pollen to other flowers. The pollen sticks to their bodies when they land on a flower. The pollen rubs onto other flowers as the bird or insect moves from plant to plant.

pollen

Bees help move pollen from flower to flower.

Pollen sticks easily to their fuzzy bodies.

Blowing pollen

Wind can also spread pollen. It blows flowers and moves their pollen to other flowers. Plants such as pine trees have cones that make pollen. The wind blows the pollen to other pine cones.

pollen

pinecone

Flowers of catkin plants hang down from branches. The wind can easily catch their pollen and blow it to other plants.

New flowers grow

A flower makes seeds with the pollen from another flower. Some flowers make only a few seeds. Other flowers make many seeds, such as the poppy flower.

seeds

seeds

Some seeds fall from flowers to the ground. Other seeds are blown far from their flowers by the wind. New flowers will grow where the seeds land.

Flowers to fruit

Flowers on some plants make **fruit**. The seeds of the plant are found in its fruit. The fruit protects the seeds.

seeds

seeds

Apples are a fruit that grow from flowers on an apple tree. Apples have seeds inside them. When apples fall to the ground, the fruit rots away. The seeds then grow into new apple trees.

Words to know and Index

buds 8–9, 10

fruit 22–23

nectar 12–13

petals 10–11

pollen 14–19

seeds 5, 15, 20–21, 22–23

sepals 8, 9

Notes for adults and an activity

Review main concepts from book with readers, including:

• What is a flower's job?
(A flower's job is to make seeds.)

• How is pollen spread? (Insects, birds, and other animals spread pollen. The wind also spreads pollen.)

• How do flowers attract insects, birds, and other animals? (Brightly colored petals, sweet smells, and nectar)

• **Designer Flowers**

This activity combines science and creative thinking. Children will take on the role of an insect, bird, or other animal that moves pollen from flower to flower. Children will create a flower designed to appeal to their senses. Ask children to consider the following questions: What is your favorite color? What is your favorite smell? What is your favorite food? Children will draw a picture of their flower and write a description of the characteristics that would attract them to the flower.

Learning more

Books

The Life Cycle of a Flower (The Life Cycle Series) by Molly Aloian and Bobbie Kalman. Crabtree Publishing Company (2004)

What is Pollination? (Big Science Ideas) by Bobbie Kalman. Crabtree Publishing Company (2011)

Websites

The Great Plant Escape: Children team up with Detective LePlant to explore how a plant grows.
http://urbanext.illinois.edu/gpe/index.cfm

Trees are Terrific... Travels with Pierre: This engaging site from the University of Illinois examines how plants change throughout the seasons.
http://urbanext.illinois.edu/trees1/index2.html